Shaniah
12-18-2017

COMMUNITY GARDEN

FOR LONELY GIRLS

FOR LONELY GIRLS

COMMUNITY GARDEN

Christine Shan Shan Hou

COMMUNITY GARDEN

GRAMMA POETRY

FOR LONELY GIRLS

Shaniah —
with love + light
x

Christine Shan Shan Hou

ISBN 978-1-5323-2706-3 FIRST PRINTING

COMMUNITY GARDEN FOR LONELY GIRLS

BY CHRISTINE SHAN SHAN HOU

DISTRIBUTED BY SMALL PRESS DISTRIBUTION WWW.SPDBOOKS.ORG

PUBLISHED BY GRAMMA POETRY WWW.GRAMMA.PRESS

I. COMMUNITY GARDEN FOR LONELY GIRLS

Light switches fade into the sides of cliffs
Eponymous flower, fortunate friend
Motherchild ascends from the womb and into outer space
Beware of linkage when tempting ancestors on battlegrounds
Even my ancestors' ghosts have ghosts!
Beware of lab coats worn by men in black clothes
Beware of men and dogs traveling in swarms to eviscerate the needy

Middle child on the beach with a tampon string dangling
between her legs
Her pubic hair glowing from the drugs
The air thick and moist with old blood of darlings
All my ancestors stand in front of a silver screen
like a tribunal
What they stand for is mercurial, material
They grow and stretch
2 limbs become 4 and 4 limbs become 8
Thus the limits of adaptation
I clasp my hands tightly behind my back
Puff out my chest for intimidation
I am neither entirely good nor humble on the tarmac
When I was a child I thought
I would have to live in a bubble
I could never ease my own mania

My mother could not protect me
A game show contestant spins a glimmering wheel
emblazoned with numbers
and I am terrified!
Even my split ends have split ends!
The sun palpitating inside my chest
Not from pleasure, but anxiety
My place in the food chain

To all my loves
Drop globules of fat down my gullet
I want to choke on your grease
Who is out of whose league?
To all my loves
I want to fuck you until our eyes
turn brighter than snow
I tilt my white ass keenly
over the bedpost
I open myself in the moonlight.
Hello round snow

Middle child
imitating an insect's immature form
Duping men in white lab coats
An insect's antennae sense the silver screen
It sounds like TA-TA-TA-TA
My arms tingle when my elbows point backwards

The traffic on Canal Street is a nightmare
My mother and father
are a nightmare
My yoga teacher sounds like TA-TA-TA-TA

Light switches fade into the sides of cliffs
while my ancestors watch from below
Middle children cry and throw themselves
off the sides of cliffs by the dozens
Chrysanthemums are holy
A girl is holy
I am a good daughter

All I want is to be slightly
better than the worst

possible outcome,
a higher judge

a sturdy, muscular foot
Once the body begins to move

it will develop a front end,
a mouth with human teeth

that opens exactly into
a 45-degree angle

Something horrible happens
in the exhibit's moat, a boy,

a gorilla won't die from
suicide or natural causes

I know I could die, but if
I could be anything

I would be an aquarium full of
colorful fish and deep

breathing,
You know

like nude and
without age

All I want is to be here
but differently

During gala season with all its fresh flowers
armored in cheap metals

and a pendulum dipped in beeswax
hating the glow of the setting sun

What does it feel like to be the sun mad with grief?
Where a father and daughter set themselves on fire

And the brightness of the summer nights
lick the planets clean

We made collages
orchid hats with little plum mouths
waxy arms bending towards hips
Dancers in wide white pants
gallantly walking towards the park
My memories of summer unwinding
meticulous spinning
Cayuga Way, Keats Road
Driving from one dead person to another
the circle rotating, creating an endless blue vacuum
a secret hiding place
What is under your wallpaper?
        a private beach?
        an almond croissant?

Everything else is reckless—dreamless, plastic and nostalgic
fern fronds unfurling
marzipan cats marching
readers snapping their beaks all the while walking

"Jabbering event" being the wrong words for the occasion
the lacking place
with its crumbling corners and billowy composites
impregnated with blue for swimming pools
save the greens for garnishes

I remember a bulbous hornet's nest
hanging from the side porch light
trumping sentimentality like an alien
The semi-solution was to go inside
            a private encounter
            an evening of philosophical toys
(Everyone cranked until their arms were sore!)
despite the lack of kitchen space
There were garlic cloves and onions hanging in dainty nets
spoons with tiny holes filled with vodka
modestly drooping houseplants
My sex swaying and swaggering
It's hard to live in another person's context
let alone as a recluse in a pastry shell

This is my feel-good position and this my feelie bag
If the cinematic impression escapes you
hold the onion tightly against your chest when taking the train back
whilst the engine slowly husks away at the horizon
however temporary or utopian it may be
Odd plaster shapes piled up to the sky
Even odder, today is the hottest day of the year
But my goal is to surrender
My body, an unwieldy pedestal with eyebrows overgrown
like the wildflowers on Antelope Island

If only I could grow upward, I would never drown.
A kite rich penny-pinch.
Some salad to suck it all in tremendously.
A sinking belly turned upside down is a rising whale.
There are allergies in tree pollen and wanting.
My disguise sat with me closely that evening.
Towards fruit and utopian metaphors.
But this is not for me.
Complaints of tough skin and bitterness.
A little less rock, a little less hardened.

The snack box option for today's flight is savory.
All salad is believable, wild.
A raised wooden walkway winding though supple, tangled wood.
Fingers persuasively holding onto two European travelers.

A crab side-walked into a hole for dinnertime.
Was it two years since Antelope Island?
Hold fork lines against the horizon and I will make it there disguised.
Sand cannot be charmed.
I poke at plantain balls, buttery and delicious.
Life is not real or for sale, even if I lay beneath the sun indefinitely.

Even if I reminisce, mildly, of discomforting fruit,
or of trees making the wind blow.
Pins and needles make a wishful fist.
Cauliflower makes me float after swallowed and forgotten.
My mother is clean and unshaven even though I may not see her naked.

With the invention of plastic, did everything all of a sudden feel cheaper
    or more light and efficient?
Mine is a headache with no end in sight.
Families are layered to look like appealing cake.
Peel off your tights before taking a nap.
You will feel the humidity as soon as you sit up.
Pep your step with green beans and coupons.
Water makes the day wetter, makes your step sprightlier.

Not dietary, but parts of a jigsaw puzzle.
A coupon scavenger with aquamarine fists jives and slips.
Salad dressing on salty lips.
A bean, a drop, and a luminescent pickle.
My mother could not draw this, nor would she want to.

I imagine a school of very tiny fish.
One of them is yellow, circular, and has a bloated belly.
I stare at her as if she is pregnant.
One has a venomous anal spine, texture like brain.
Recyclable plastic is the dream that I mean.
I tear through a strung picture curtain jubilantly.
I am wild for them without insides.

A cyborg never grins because it has no mother tongue.

Take no lemon squares to the beach.
Sand cannot get into its machinery.
Memory's mechanism is tender.

BECOMING ALL BODY IS NOT WHAT MY MOTHER TAUGHT ME

There is paranoia in immigration.
Clamoring fruits in the kitchen.
I am speaking of red apples, sliced and without skin.
Ever since puberty I have experienced an increased desire to be swaddled.
Called euphoria backwards.
Cereal is more expensive when not on sale.
I am allowed three options.

Hair, when out of my face is more acceptable.
Make tight or loose around the waist.
Three generations under one suspicious roof.
The untidiness of intention mixed with the grueling nature of doubt.

Dreamed my plants turned plastic.

Dreamed I refused my own shell.

A house duster is a barbarian muffler.

You must wait thirty minutes after eating
before swimming or running around the mall.
I did it once and threw up everywhere.
Not from playing 'Mother May I' or
from shopping.
What did you say?
Sad salad. A sad fish in a salad.

AUTOBIOGRAPHICAL SONG

Trimmings made of milk and nuts.
Tighter, and not all boyish.
Girly boy wakes up wet anyway.
Once antagonized by delicate lace,
you cannot control which direction
childhood wanders towards.
A classical arrangement is never fit
or tidy because mushrooms grow around it.
I adore its pungent and irresponsible nature.

A turtle, Mott Senior, swims further out to sea.
His home is threatened by sunscreen.
The chance for otherness is not an option.
Mother tongue hide from the sun.
Make a curly toe at the end of a line
of crooked ones.

I play with ants on the red kitchen carpet.
One climbs on my thumb.
Better not to distract him from his busy day
at the wallpaper factory.
I could only have fish as pets.

Dried leaves stuffed into an orange plastic bag make
a smiling pumpkin.
Language is wild and radiant to the bone.
Lucky sea glass found amongst a scattering of pennies.
My legs feel greasy in the hot sun.

I turn on and off and on and off while pushing your buttons.

INSTRUCTIONS FOR LUCID DREAMING

Keep a look out for light switches because
they don't work in dreams. Neither do telephones.
Focus on your physical sensations. Emphasize
simplicity, sincerity, and brotherly love.
Symbolism is my only disguise. Dreaming is
a way of shedding unhealthy wishes.
I am helpless like a crumpled car.

Running in a square should not be confused
with sluttin' around. A bicycle for laundry does
not have backwards brakes. Mound of forgotten
keys turns hot in my pants. It gets better after
the hair is pulled off my face. Neither witch nor
cyborg makes the dream heard. If I lay here,
how long will I lay here?

Mushrooms grow around me and into my brain.
A large orgiastic pile of women build a colony
called Foodtown. Make sure to scan your card
for extra savings. Be wary of the thunderstorm
in the salad bar. A little burn goes a long way,
but not if you run out of batteries
while defending your art.

"Hair-mmm-hair" my mother says when feigning interest. Sometimes an everyday expression can sound slightly comical. No sex talk radio after ten o'clock. The decision to bend identity congregates elsewhere. Toss a salad into the air and the universe will catch it. Because I have small ear holes, I have always had trouble fitting wires into them. Information goes into me via a green bicycle lane. Psychology blazes ahead at full force on glittering grass. I used to wish to be called sir. My mother is not a cyborg, nor does she determine my friendships (which are not sisterhood). Even if they involve women in large circle skirts spinning. Even if the large circle is a basketball hoop suspended over a rotten driveway. A basketball rolls down the street and into a crowded mall. There is not enough fiction in shopping to make it a collaborative experience. Is painting a women's sport? Sports bring people close together, while art about sports brings people closer. A closeted space does not warm quickly. The roof leaks at the corners, but I stuff coupons into its holes. Too many babies and you will be asked to leave the house.
Mother, not a hippie.

DISRUPTED MATERIAL (FOUR-HAND SPECIAL)

Enough beef didacticism, all the girls are doing it.
Crispiness makes its way into the center.

A complaint seldom explodes after the expiration date.

I cough into a cushion.
It turns into a soft piece of cake.

Crushed velvet on the floor
blossoms beneath my mother's feet.

A ferocious jungle approaches Customs.
I spiral a little while wrapped in fur.

Drink, don't slurp when eating hot pot.
Seek solace in a house duster.

The car flew over the guardrail and landed in the Bronx Zoo.
Three generations killed just like that.

It's between the haves and have-nots.

What dying has never felt so windy.

The kitchen is my unnamed diary. I am digging for
meat with unkempt fingernails. Fruit can be eaten
in public, while lobster should only be eaten in private.
Sex is to snuggling as heaven is to purgatory, swallow
a couple of pills for the headache. All I need are radio
voices, soft and sweet. Do you want me to hold you or
let you be free? The adoration of fact hesitates suddenly.
Catholic ceremonies are the most depressing.
Titanium white erases chandelier and wound.
I would never treat my American Girl doll like that!
Up close, farther, further. The watch broke as he put it
on my wrist. It was my birthday.
I have never built a shrine nor do I see myself doing so.
Rub wood for freedom, rub wood for luck.
Flavorful bread lights up my eyes.
Enough dilly-dallying. The love is coming.

You stare at me like a wide-eyed
monkey. Abstraction of the face begins
here occasionally moving to the backseat.
If I concentrate hard enough I can hear
voices stirring inside the reproductive
organs of plants. A lawn weed that is
an itty-bitty pussy trap. An itty-bitty
pussy trap makes me white and fat,
like stinky cheese stuffed into a blanket.
Weather is satisfaction when dressed for the
occasion. I encourage you to pay attention
to geographies moving through the body,
dreams vacillating between foreign and familiar.
There is a cage suspended above my writing
desk. A burden that releases me kindly into
space, like clouds gyrating slower than the
senses. Dolphins swim away
from each other above the Esopus Creek.
Oh golden age of television!
Let it be full of fossils.

Hypnosis brings out my science fiction.
Why do I have a psychotic urge to smile?
Certain colors can be blinding.
I use my fingers to touch myself and then
waste the smell unapologetically.
What mother would approve an odorless
disguise? The girl in the milk aquarium
could never swim away. I know because
I was there and watched her rolling all of the
autobiographies in the world into a giant ball.
The chatter of children is noticeably absent.
They say the basketball never erroneously
falls into the hoop. "Reality is that which,
when you stop believing in it, doesn't go away,"
said PKD. I am skeptical of such hallucinogenic
terms. I exchange triangles with a Chinese
cyborg, but never agree to the taste test. Opened
the book of a thousand eyes, felt shame from
too much knowing. Why do you ask me what
reality is? During hypnosis I held hands with
my former self and floated over the purple sea.
I grazed my fingers over the surface. Bright
orange fish stained my fingertips. A tongue
on an elegantly bent pole makes the heart
grow louder.

My amnesia is self-inflicted. Yogurt sways back and
forth inside me. I hover majestically from here to there,
through hot temperatures and high humidity. A little
white lie makes my pouch heavy. It makes its way
round and into a nice fence. An onslaught of e-mails,
slaughterhouse of spam. What about my dreams?
"You're young so you're gonna wanna fuck like bunnies,"
she said. But I still whimper in my sleep (not a girly boy).
I make it out in a quick and queer zigzag, hypothetically.
The truth is I want to be a hippie in a circle skirt.
I lack the proper amount of testosterone to make decisions.
I take butter in my tea. I may be doomed to repeat myself,
but it is my backyard, not yours.

If two words are not paired correctly
The imbalance creates waves of discomfort
in its users. A city of crystals becomes what
you least expect. Thick-skinned and unruly.
And tradition: let it be burned at the stake.
A diagnosis is questioned and then questioned
again. Single men gather in a comfortable zone
at the base of the tree where electricity comes out.
It frightens you. This is why you should never
go after just one exposed prey, but a pack, because
the element of surprise is scarce. Ordinary death
is just that, ordinary. Theoretically damaged people
should not care about sex, but they do.
The religious fear of evil can itself lead to evil.
Do a good deed and throw it into the sea.
Do not expect a reward or a diagnosis.
Do not diagnose theoretically damaged
people and then enter them into databases.
The element of surprise is sentience.

Ordinary feelings require melodramatic status.
A driveway cannot expect sympathy especially
if it is rotten and surrounded by invasive species.
I dream sporadically of reincarnation. I wet myself
thinking about the possibility. In movies, wounded
female birds attract fancy men. The brown bird of reality
is the true vacillator. A love story is told with a razorblade
tucked beneath its tongue. Sometimes I am alarmed by
the facts it produces. Most of the time I accept them.
To rub up against someone else's love is dangerous.
Even if the feeling is mutual one must take into account
vocation. A vocation does not always have a place.
A vacation usually does, mine is a melting shopping
mall where I encounter a corporate water fountain,
an enormous green globe glistening like a peeled grape.
I throw pennies at it until it explodes. How easy it is to
confuse irresponsible behavior for radical politics,
incurable mania, witchy spells, etc.
Goodnight self, my goddess is dimming.

Not reincarnation, but gym class. First the arms and then the tails.
I am a small, Chinese girl, therefore picked last. I enter into the game
fluidly, albeit surgically, and with precision. "You are only as strong
as your weakest girl," announces the woman on TV with a smirk
and a wink. Not to mention all the children could see my fish whistle.
Who is the judge here? One size fits all eggs therefore one size must
fit all babies. Cauliflower is meaningful and versatile, although
it is off-white, a sad color description missing a face. The news is never
far behind. It's the trapdoor beneath the basketball that worries me.

Smash garlic with my fist.
I am cured thanks to the feng shui lady.
I am wearing a dainty apron tied around my
waist and a wig made of leaves, a fistful of mushrooms
in my left hand. I sense the suspicion is mutual.
All troubles have to roll somewhere and on to something.
In this case from my neighbor's house onto my front lawn.
Then the feng shui lady says there is too much water in me
and my sisters. Mildly offended, I tell her it is not a popularity
contest. The color quickly darkens on my mood ring. I must be
hungry. I devour a plate of country style green bean sheet jelly.
Gluten flows through me like green slime. I jam my finger in
the hole to stop it. This, too, is a passing feeling.
I shower everyday to wash the excess color down the drain.

Living with hard water has been hard on my hair.
I keep my mother tongue in my mouth to look less creepy.

I peruse biographies of queer, literary figures from the early
20th century in hopes of stimulating my situation. Ding!
The kitchen timer goes off. I open the oven door and to my
surprise it starts an earthquake in China. It endangers the lives
of school children but sets the zoo animals free. I imagine their
small voices and then weep for the children quickly and efficiently.
My inner creature does not stumble. Healthy wishes struggle to escape
through the open window. Otherwise all is alive and well on this end.
I am chopping vegetables to juice when all of a sudden I am
overcome by vertigo from a passing thought about the universe.
Ding! Uncover and fluff. The rice is ready!

Take a deep breath and adjust privacy settings
filled with pills of different shapes and colors.
I stretch my feet and crack my toes, which have become
stiff from last night's sleepwalking. I take vitamins not
out of necessity but my doctor's only suggestion.
There's a difference in theory, not practicality. I'm sorry
I can't make it to your opening, but my oven has been
overgrown with mushrooms. There's plenty of time to
become more socially disciplined. Singularity decreases
my appetite. I treat myself with an easy green salad at
the royal history buffet. I want to believe there is enough
good energy to go around to everyone, so I get in the car
and drive upstate.

There's my boss walking towards me on her hands.
There she is again saving me from a thousand angry bees.
I rip off my clothes and flee down the driveway.
A sad outfit, now filled with bees.
No garment just feathers.

"I'm not a Peter Pan boy, I do plenty of grown-up things!"
My lover insists as he reaches for my ass. Instead he takes
a pair of tweezers and pulls a splinter from my knee.
All trouble wants to start somewhere—I learn this lesson
the slow way, by rolling. Trees begin to insert themselves
into my peripheral vision, roughly one per hour. Daylight
transgresses evening's billow. An alarming light
shines through my window and into my left eyeball.
The leaves are made of plastic.
The lobster mushrooms taste like lobster.

I. COMMUNITY GARDEN FOR LONELY GIRLS

II. FAMILY TEACHINGS

TO MAKE SURE THAT MATTERS ARE INTELLECTUALLY DEALT WITH, ONE MUST NOT BE EMOTIONAL IN MAKING THE RIGHT DECISION.

The mind is an emotional orb. The disaster is forthcoming and cannot be anticipated. The mind sinks one thousand ways. What is frightening some of the time can be frightening all of the time. The same goes for tomorrow. Who we are today is not who we are tomorrow. This is why we must churn, or be churned. Standing up for one's self is not the same as walking without a destination. A journey is necessary in order to become a SELF-MADE MAN. Feelings aside, what do I hope to achieve in such a short amount of time—the right to certainty?

WHEN PEOPLE ARE IN CONVERSATION, DON'T SPEAK IN THE MIDST OF THEIR TALK.

We talk over each other all the time. We exchange ghosts in the details. The ghosts are made up of oranges. All bent out of shape after interrupting a single thought. How does an orange dinner sound to you? At the beginning of a nation, fear surrounds the things you love. And though I am not defined by what I love, I believe I am defined by what I fear. I am scared most of the time. I crouch in the corner facing the wall. In the middle of the conversation, I am airlifted over a sea of freaks. *The ancient Chinese believe the spirit of all dead ancestors must be catered so as to avoid any angry ghosts in the family.* And the crime doesn't stop there.

DON'T DISCUSS SERIOUS MATTER WITH THE MERE ACQUAINTANCE.

My grandfather, Hou Kang Hua, was arrested in 1961 at three o'clock in the morning. Unable to collect any clothes or supplies, he was blindfolded and forced to board a plane to Sikkim, then transported on horseback to the border. There, he was forced to cross through the Himalayan Mountains via the Nathu La. Nathu means "listening ears" and La means "pass." He follows a mailman to Tibet, waist-deep in snow, never to be seen again.

Blood is thicker than water
An arrangement made by God
Treacherous is the land that devours the needy
To whom do you belong?
The states

TO AVOID SUSPICION, BE SURE PLUMES ARE PROTECTED.

I stretched alone for miles, voiceless and with braided birds overhead. Whose dream am I immortal in? I am surrounded by ugly floral wallpaper. All the flowers giving me the evil eye. To come to the conclusion: We are all alone in this world. Nothing but meat remains. It takes time to be known. Immortality is not the end point. The seeming abundance of wealth and fortune has no basis in today's technology. I appear smaller and smaller on the passageway. A pale form, neglected. Submission as a form of protection. *To have no lineage will be without the basic social protection.*

Everybody lies a little bit here and there

ALWAYS WASH OR HAVE A BATH BEFORE GOING TO BED FOR THE NIGHT; BED MUST BE KEPT CLEAN TO HAVE A PROPER REST.

I am obedient when it comes to sleep. Haunting is at its prime in the after hours. The search for clarity needs no explanation. Envisioned the heartless in respect to the gainfully employed. SELF-MADE MAN leaves me clear in my need for queer and clean.

TO THE KIND HEARTED SHOW PROPER RESPECT, TO THE WICKED KEEP FAR AWAY.

An oblong shadow cast over a tumult that is the self. Perhaps it is extinction that we fear the most. The drought always in front of us is as present as ever. Experience shrivels leaving behind a pile of skin. Skin, what we see in the mirror—that which envelops us. The majesty of our insides reveals the slow manipulation of hormones. The everyday spinning us in circles so fast we emit light. Light, being what we need the most. We throw light on desire. We throw desire into a hole. And the rest is history. Or so we think. But there is still a ways to go—several more border wars. Children are tucked into bed; curtains are drawn tightly shut. Our commitment, our grasping for the unreal defines us. This hot and sticky core implanted in the center of our beings. What's gray stays gray. The kingdom of tomorrow awaits us all. There is no need for God—at least not now.

I stand before my ancestral tribe muttering words to myself. All the words I say in one day reap no benefit for the outsider. I clear out my nasal passages over old meat. The circumstances will change, but the mindset will not.

Living free
in this world
inflicts just the
right amount of
cruelty

ONE MUST NOT FIGHT FOR THE CENTER SEAT DON'T WALK IN THE MIDDLE.

My great-grandfather, Hou Chin Hsiu, was arrested in 1963. Crammed into a train with the word "enemy" scrawled along the side of it. He was taken to the Deoli Internment camp in Rajasthan. And though the war technically lasted for one month, he was interned for the next six years.

As the train rode through the countryside, men threw sticks and rocks at it.

Humiliation quiets us in the realm of uncertainty.

Go back.

Defeat knows no bounds. Miraculously, a contradiction appears within shelter of the deep blue lake. Between two countries: a maw for the deported.

Understand that my behavior has no limits. It stretches infinitely. Muscle tied to muscle. I live within the terror of boxes to come. When time is not on our side, but above the translucent gray.

Beauty knows no terror
The transgression is real
Listening ears
Botched medical procedure
Lineage
The custodian of enemy property takes it all

WHEN UNPREDICTABLE THINGS HAPPEN BE CALMED, DON'T GIVE AWAY FAKE ASSURANCE OR FALSE HOPE TO OTHERS.

The better to see you. "Unlikeable" being the least bit of your worries. If you have the right idea, the talisman will guide you. But what is seeing when we are set up for failure in the dunes of lust? Tears whither our bodies into submission. This is the moment where truth unfolds. This is where you will be set free. An almost touching occurs. We touch in blue spirit, woven into the context of contemporary. Era flashes its earthly glow. Wandering naked on all fours. This floor is the closest to my state of being. An individual hormone is hardly benign. Throughout history, we have been hopelessly dedicated to the bad habits that make us animals. But why tradition? Why now?

TRUTH SHALL MAKE YOU FREE, GO AFTER IT.

Absorbed by feeling for a second time. What if truth is not a destination, but the mountains? How far did you travel to make it here? It is easy to get hurt when crossing borders. The skull tossed back and forth like a ball. Abstraction not as erasure, but legitimate moments in time. City perched above the natural grain. Frustrated by red graves planted in the middle. What we already have in possession, we cannot gain. Tradition throws light at the wrong point of focus. Look into the screen. Telecommunication is vital.

RECIPROCATE THE FAVOR YOU HAVE RECEIVED.

Don't look the monkey directly in the eye. Thoughtful communication can unknowingly strike fear into a creature's heart. An apron is tied around the statue's waist to protect the soul. Despite "looking-glass shame," corpses of two dead stars reciprocate favors. Round friends at a ghost-filling station. The teeth of oranges. The oranges of the mind spiraling in aching regret.

Return to the money of madness
Equal and penetrable
Despite the cool
white veil.

ALWAYS RESPECT AND TALK POLITELY TO THE PERSON OLDER THAN YOU.

Hold your germs close to your obedient mouth. This is not about the self, rather its proximity to nationhood. Blind lead the blind into unspeakable distances. Paying homage to the dead is the same as trembling before a feeding frenzy.

How does one mourn
the loss of sight
the states

DON'T SPEAK ABOUT THE WEAKNESS OF OTHERS; NEVER SHOW OFF YOUR STRENGTH AND WEALTH.

Pay respect to
the thin façade
of their maleness

DON'T USE ROUGH AND HARSH WORDS WHEN DEALING WITH PEOPLE IN DIFFICULTY.

Beasts are humbled by sex and seek the clarity of an egg white. Whom do we turn to in search of vibrations? Round friends. Staggered trees. They were pruned so aggressively, yet their shapes weren't something we pretended to know. An obscure need supplanted itself in the middle of the forest. How thick is the admission of guilt? Condensed milk.

REMEMBER ITS SOURCE WHILE DRINKING THE WATER.
LEAVES FALL TO RETURN TO ROOT.

Switch your clasp. Bring the opposite thumb on top. Comfort defines our being on this earth. And so discomfort unnerves us, stiffens our muscles. Are we geniuses? Are we babies? The past left for dead, the dead left to fend for themselves. Songs about childhood are kept for safekeeping in the spine. And the paintings of life say so much about us. So what do we crave? Illusions.

Without protection
the virus spreads
from cell to cell
from moon to moon

I. COMMUNITY GARDEN FOR LONELY GIRLS

II. FAMILY TEACHINGS

III. MEN DYING FOR WEALTH, BIRDS DYING FOR FOODS

Hakka people like animal offal a lot.
Hakka people improve their portal skills over holiday.

Hakka people spew scintillating data all over the playing field.
Multi-dimensional crystals shine anxiously too.

Big girls in prison wait for what they want to want them back.
They read and read until they go blind and then die like the desert.

Dutiful daughter points her camera at the country.
She has no European travels.

There are archival limits when it comes to pleasure.
Wedge used to prop a door open is a sliding scale for memories

One feels especially strong for being American.
Descriptions are equal insofar as bodies are equal.

Dressed in sequined devotional attire,
spill everything you own into a swamp.

MODERN COMPETITORS

Inside an arena for hide and seek
is the secret to solitude.

Questioning suspects is a lengthy
process. One that can take hours,

days, even weeks. The question:
"What are you?" generating a more

positive response than: "What's
wrong with you?" Is it true that

we only root for the outnumbered?
There is safety in numbers, but once

the threat has abated it's every
competitor for them selves.

The interception of deities resembles
malice at its most unspeakable terms.

All one can do is watch the carnage.
Protect the senses with dazzling devices

and a spine made of steel. Submission
viewed not as failure but a reticulate

process bound by a natural band of light.
Narcissism is a heat-sensing organ

excited by the spoils of girlhood.
An extra level of testosterone

may lead to an unfair advantage
but the definition of female oppresses

like a heat wave in the middle of
August, domelike and aching.

Do you need a voice of soft reason?
Try mystical persuasion
Act like a nun in the presence of elders.
Act without acting out.
I am an anima woman.
I am young and pliable.
I flower into the strangeness of myself.
Voluptuous sea creature
divine in theory, but beached and about to explode
on the shorelines of Northern Canada
Where my cousins hide
in a remote cabin by a lake.
My cousin,
You step into the cabin but leave your wings
outside
You are whole.
You were never whole.
You are partially whole.
You are one-third whole.
You are whole-hearted.
You are sewed into your clothes
inside-out.
You are the memory of the echo of God's voice
when He says: GO TO HELL.

A scattering soul needs a variety of small devices.
Wires, rather miracles, connect children
to dark systems.
Electricity comes into them,
Still they do not bend.
Crying is part of it.
Self-control is part of it.
The mind-cure movement is part of it.
THAT WHICH MEN LIVE FOR is part of it.
But demonstrates poor alignment
Exercise self-control when walking towards men.
The power of suggestion is a wet blanket
eating itself out.
Hastily, I vacuum the flower from the stem,
suck the snail from the shell
Take, take, take!
My friend streams forth from the television
and holds a mirror to the divided self.
Our potential love affair ends the conversation
So I re-crystallize myself around this moment
And the conversation becomes general.
My cousin, my friend, I believe you are an angel too.
I believe you are put on this earth to frighten the wolves
of sensibility.
I BELIEVE GOD HEARS YOU.
You are small.
You are small like dust in all the small places.

BUBBLE

—FOR BRANDON

A bubble pops spilling its juices all over the table.

A mountain yawns, contaminating the rest of the air.

The mountain is a mountain of iguanas.
I worship it, an exercise from ancient days.

0

I rent a hole to rest inside and open my heart chakra.
See how the size of the hole does not matter,
rather its ontological purpose, how it looks in pictures,
its crumbling façade.

I prepare soup in the hole
Then boil away the broth

There are young demons in the hole. I fight them with my
hands without knowing what they have done to deserve it.
I sweat and gather more fighting materials.
No swords. They were not in the budget.

0 0
0

Because I read

Instruction manuals

Religious iconography

Activity statements

I am tired in dreams

Humiliation by iguanas and oracles

Friend ships

Indigestion

Limits adaptation

Policemen follow the drama

0 0 0

0 0

Recall the necessary outlets
when dreaming towards the mountaintop.
Carry my pets there
Martyr flesh for flesh

Dine on cream and jerky and keep on floating
Scout for shimmering pleasures beneath rocks.
Hope not to rot so the vast sequence
of events can unfold in its entirety.
Can I achieve the right ratios?
How about when fucking?
A little rock shoved into a hole
The radiant bits all but radiant
like snow
in a glove

0 0 0 0
0 0 0

I arrive at the top and pull all the stops.
I put on a sweetheart dress
to relieve me from my journey's suffering.
Hold a magnifying glass up to my nipples.
Predict a disaster:
NO LOVE IN THE MONTH OF JUNE

Rub synthetic bovine gall bladder
all over the inside of my mouth.
Stuff me.

Fast relentlessly, but stay hydrated.

I open my legs and a saint comes out
like a tiny blessing.

0 0 0 0 0

0 0 0 0

What is this mission
that I'm after?
Is it finding the hole
inside of me and falling
through it
triumphantly
naked
while reasoning
with fingers
and star
voices
that drain me
until my death?

Each reason in its own bubble.

Each reason is trying to outweigh another reason in its own bubble.

0 0 0 0 0 0

0 0 0 0 0

TO THE WICKED KEEP FAR AWAY

I'm all for the surgical arrangements of plastic lips
On doves flying into the dark corners of my heart.

Where a worm curls into a feeding position and stays there.
I let my bodywash beads drain into the ocean breeding toxic roe.

By now the color of money has flooded the whole face of the ocean.
Hand-tinted yellow sending energy in the form of extra yellow.

My boyfriend's kumquats turn from orange to yellow to white.
I store them in a dark cabinet like shrinking-gut-trophies and admire them.

I fondle my guts in public, to the wicked keep far away.
Men dying for wealth, birds dying for foods.

Ask questions as big as the movies.
Teach men and woman how serious computers read minds.

A wide screen of daffodils
Like staring into a rock, hungrily.

Domestic strangers in a duplicitous duplex cure each other.
When one of the strangers says: "I learned the hard way."

I made this so that you could come out of your stomach obediently.
A surplus of daffodils becomes an emergency garland.

A boy cuts off his genitals because he doesn't want them.
If you don't want the sunset throw it into the sewer.

MY BODILY CONCEPTION OF FAITH IS STERILE AND UNSCENTED

All technology can offer us are new options as to how to behave in an
  imaginary realm.
Not all waiting is the same version of the story.

For instance, you can wait for your creation to come to life and love you
more than you could ever love it.

Another luring scent on an abandoned park bench.
Fingerprints gone missing from emollients.

The danger of saying things anonymously as quick as a slit to the uterus.
The repetition of the everyday, flatlands that mock us for the foreseeable future.

We are all guilty of thinking something terrible.
Like, what if you deserve the crime you are given?

Skin puckers over a hole to seal in past objects.
Behind my face, something hexagonal bobs up and down in stormy waters.

When you look with my eyes what do you see?
A kneeling monkey inside a jungle-shrouded temple.

Schoolchildren are marching in and out of a museum.
It is bad luck to leave dead fruit inside any building, inhabited or not.

I have learned to take certain precautions with the unwillingness of fools.
Glamour is a fragile phenomena—I inch my way near it.

Of indeterminate crystals and shock, where does one look?
Sweat beads down into a nearby lake, a blinking phantasm.

War tears at the brawn of a country's struggle for existence.
The recovery of antiquities reveals the cracks on a dutiful face.

A god falls from the sky and is reduced to blood antiquity.
How criminal the world looks in ultraviolet.

THE SIGN FOR "KILLING" IS ONE HAND SLIDING BENEATH THE OTHER: THE BALLAD OF HARUNA YUKAWA

You are told that you are not a flower
You are convinced you are the reincarnation

of a Japanese female spy in World War II
WHY ARE YOU HERE?

Even the oddest situation produces a desert
But what if you become a bargaining chip

Save yourself, don't save yourself
Your mother is waiting for you

An authentic experience of burning
Fragrant eclipse

Pieces of the ceiling come crashing down
and fall into the angry mob

before turning into mud
Still you do not blink in the mirror

of life
of invasion

of men and women in an assembly line
Moving their limbs in unison

They bulge harmonious inside a white factory
Plotting a land without masculinity

A cloud passes by and is quickly snorted
That's when you begin to shrink

You feel betrayed when the season changes
A stone's throw from the fence

The woman you thought you were disappeared into the desk
Only the sweater remains

The device will duplicate your mind and place it into an egg
Yet you fear the thinness of being

The look on your face is the constraint
Of your face

One sex a day for the rest of the days
Flirting mindlessly into the desert

Sand flits across your face
You cannot shake off what you think happened to you

So you swallow the marriage whole
Fallopian tubes bloom in your abandoned bedroom

A silk rope slides out of your window
A corpse slides underneath a rock

White fence slowly makes its way around the house
with green curtains

Behind, a girl methodically strokes herself in the bay window
You are inconsolably tied to your journey

Covert
Like a cat with a dead bird tied around its neck

:

Cloud face
Golden trimming

Manicure mansion
Valley finger

Ghostly piano
Uncanny organ

Funeral throne
Abnormal arboretum

:

Just like the olden days
when you used to wake up

next to your wife and peered
with one eye into the wood

IMMIGRATION SONG

The boy bends so far backwards he looks
like he wants death, but he is a pretender
I peer into his mouth's horizon
There are crabs scuttling across rocks
The opposite direction of where I should be looking
I play with ants and wait for the circus
I spin backwards in circles, crashing into walls
My circles get smaller and smaller until they become
baby circles, then just a baby
Baby pours out of arms
Baby declares autonomy, eats fatty pork
on Chinese New Year
On the other side of the country, a trapeze artist falls
to her death
Fat is no salvation in Los Angeles
Here comes Animus to strike me
Magic wand = transformation
Ants vibrate on the kitchen floor without water
Hair flows from the faucet, casting an ominous shadow
I pick out eveningwear based on these circumstances
The best haircut for a sweetheart neckline is no hair

Erase the memory and then the eyes,
Then instantly match the movement of your neighbor.
Facial recognition systems lull people into a false sense of security.
Just like that, identities melt away into the blue.
Everyday the kids get a little wilier,
Hitching rides with strangers.
Nothing to snack on but a mealy apple that has been sitting out for weeks.
To live and sleep amongst your prey
Here's how to do the flowers
Play host at the dinner party
Then play Russian roulette
When restoring the hard drive, intuitively scan the cursor over the largest form
Apply ointment to the exterior
Allow the form to dictate direction, but not the other way around.
Install every fear into your worst enemy.
One for men
And one for women
Stuck in a place where you don't want to be
Now having to deal with wild pigs
The refugees have no choice but to change their tactics.
Gather in large numbers for a totally different flying technique
Streamlined and energy efficient

Let's travel together
Safely
On hoverboards
Over countries
The same old story
From rags to riches
Apply the cool gel of disbelief
With a coffee stirrer,
Eat with a side of coffee and cake.
Imagine what part of this poem qualifies it as "junk"
Take that part and bury it outside.
A sapling
Becomes a colony
Of ants
Each ant
Instantly matching the movement of its neighbor.
A skeleton made from the bodies of 2 million workers
On payroll
Running out of space on the hard drive
For pigs
And folic acid
And car payments

Let's hear their voices!
The poem is no cause for celebration
The heir to the fortune is no cause for celebration
Don't cry

Instead hold people accountable for their mistakes.
Blow air bubbles into the margins of doubt.
Baseball field-shaped bubbles
An influx of foreign influence from the Western world
Junk mail
Another pair of sneakers
The internal bodily functions of this poem
Miniature people in human machines turn the challenges of the machine to
 their advantage
Channel super powers
Facial recognition technology
Cannot be replicated with smoke
And mirrors
A complicated meeting of cultural and spiritual matters.
Refugees constantly shift in a floating maze,
Passageways open and close in a series of unremarkable patterns.
The urgency of recognition is a desire for consistency in the modern world.
Desire having no real consequences
When it's fight-or-flight
And nourishment is scarce
And the leaves
The leaves
Are bloodless.

And sex did not create us evenly.

The fashion declines statement.

And the shit on your face is the history of delicacies.

When the disruption of hierarchy deflates us too.

The hammering of souls while sealed in fur.

And we are elated, happily along for the ride.

The cultural significance of feeling sentimental in times of catastrophe.

While navigating the meadow of hypotheticals, I tripped and broke my arm.

And the drive is incomplete without you.

What eyes?

Everyday it is dark and I am not where I want to be.

The movies.

Erotic chatter that is hardly the definition of static.

Slip hints to the bourgeois.

Home to the patriotic loon.

Fishies swimming home in the dark.

The arrival of plentiful.

Tremendous healing adapts to the matriarchy.

How do you say no to a rigorous saint?

How soon until the race is over?

We do not mourn the disruption of hierarchy because we want to be up there too.

Arrogant children ponder an open site.

A little over a pesky dozen.

Anomaly of regulars.

Emergence of a still life.

Vines grow over vines until they become forgotten by the majority.

We need to keep the history of detainment alive.

How to get there how to get there how to get here.

The problem of this body is America.

And there is an emergency in my computer.

Throw a mirror into a swamp, release a soul.

In haste, we retrieve the leftovers—they cannot be abandoned!

A flossing material.

A disguise in blood diamonds.

Material empathy overcomes the drooling child.

We sleep in the scarlet night.

Just because it is not our body, doesn't make it a finished product.

What does the vagrant want?

The role of the poet is a lie.

The history of detainment correlates with the history of natural skin.

Somewhere out in the countryside, a concept is shrinking.

The aftermath of detainment is a blank cage rattling in the desert wind.

Do we all want contemporary?

The sky opens up and we are split apart.

Armless, I emerge reckless.

Tourniquet to stop the blood rainbow.

To be reduced to hollow refuse.

A grove at the edge of a swamp provides an exit strategy.

To be held in your grave.

Water escapes through the cracks leaving the fishies to die.

The history of prison is the history of love.

We place guards around the perimeter and that is love.

Blossoming is a possibility.

You can't know if it is possible to blossom in prison if you've never been in one.

You can't know how it feels like to die.

I conceptualize a peak and my imagination goes to a valley of amputated arms.

Even the now moves with such glacial intensity.

Art is the shit on your face.

It is pain, but it is manageable.

A day job.

The movies.

The emergency of sentiment blinds us momentarily.

The beginning of tea and canaries.

Nameless creates a peculiar mound, *the mound is oddly precise.*

A battlefield of corpses is reduced to a concept.

We are reduced to a concept.

The traditional suicide of "following in death."

We cower beneath the steps of God.

Our yearning becomes material for tragedy.

A body is tied to an appeal.

Say no to the appeal.

Upset the balance and a river flows backwards into the rain.

The key of being able to live anywhere is the queen.
The trouble with saintliness is its proximity to godliness.

Destroying an entire group of invasive creatures at once
is the only way to do it. Driven out of dankness

Lone survivors fear helicopters overhead. It is impossible to know
if an invader has truly been eliminated until several years later.

Even pigs at their most mature state are not immune to tragedy.
Herding creates an impenetrable wall of stares. Within the life

of the perfect creature an idea is forced into action. The equivalent
of plucking eggs and vegetables off fertile ground where worms

spawn a disposable creature. Wreckage is necessary when forcing
any idea into action. Bystanders smother a mound of good intentions

at a gala banquet. As soon as trust wavers, erroneous puddles
promptly evaporate. The point of aging is not to fill holes but

charm untrustworthy bystanders with your determination.
You cannot offer up the women in your life as proof of your goodness.

I. COMMUNITY GARDEN FOR LONELY GIRLS

II. FAMILY TEACHINGS

III. MEN DYING FOR WEALTH, BIRDS DYING FOR FOODS

IV. THE APPARITION

At night the fruit
languished

a feast with hot milk
& dandy

soured by
what was once rock

is now office parts
missing from the cubicle

on 22nd street
the smell of waste

& urine
corrode the daily

walks of citizens to work
past the interior showcase

of beach chairs
oh look at those small

blessed objects
sitting in constructive rest

oh look at the shellfish
and their washed-up origins

the fountain that spurts
green flesh

becomes mosaic
in the aftermath of lunch

burn the darned book
& burn the office

& shatter those parts that claim
the day

& teeter along the edgy edge
of the eggy egg

& split the hairs on the pubic bone
into two

no more appetite
except for potatoes

& binary forms
dipped in fondue

of the future
composed of winners and losers

becomes nourishment
for the nest

in your brain
where a snake

levitates calmly in the air
its body becoming

more trivial by the hour
like choosing bread

at the grocery store
then slowly counting the hours until

the bread rots in your mouth
a meager feast for ancestors

their essence bottled
into detergent for cleansing

the meager fruits
of your nightly labor

& blue-blotted birds
in your silken hair, where

did they come from
& who was watching

the office
parts

The elevator goes up and my tears flow down
while the people's opinions decrease rapidly.
Chatter in the amiable distance.
We are all vegetables alone in the night
flowers in my glazed esophagus.
Tie string around the baby's wrist
:bind the soul to the body
Tie a collar around the dog's neck
:bind the body to the master
Master eats a little bit of pork for survival.
The dog consumes its complex
and it is contagious.
To sink beneath the earthly surface
and know that heaven is coming
Its existence taints us, enlists God's spells
A room that paints us into complacency
made dark and darker
brown and browner
Silence created by the mud of elders.
What goes around comes out the other ear
Scattered, predatory and baseless.
Like feral leaves in grass
Stray dogs in the distance
Myriad of slobbering tongues.

The law states:
Who you are in the morning
is not
who you are
at night
a home amongst the forbidden
a minor discrepancy
a boy being folded into the shape of a crab
shoved into a car, not a symbol.
The neighbors step out of their unseen
houses to watch as neighbors do.
It is dusk
Colors amass in a heavenly green
Prayer hands cup over prayer hands
Littles play with other littles
Little boys' genitals like hanging fruit
(The apple fills my hybrid throat with glee)
I enter into child's pose
Spill out the contents of my brain
Perform miracles in the bowels of my animal kingdom
What is it like to have another half
What is it like to have, but not own
What is it like
To look down at a pile of soft muscles and know
they are not yours
What is the feeling of new skin
The soaking of vegetables in salted water.

I would rather place a paper crown on my head
and go to sleep than give energy to a terrifying painting
It is not about what I want, but what I choose to see and how I act
Even the fragments bend themselves out of shape in an act of rebellion
There is nothing new to this sequence
Like scissors
Everyday I feel a little bit further away from where I started
A seed from inside the perspective of a melon
My studio is my restless home
My shiny apparatus is a tongue scraper with soft rubber handles
I am only half-formed myself
Like a sibyl's pathetic vegetables
I wear a braid that creates a noose at the end of it
Stay awake for the duration of the design
Throw the application into the imaginary terrain
My hormones click and then arrange to be closer to water
An artichoke has no claim to the ocean
Where are my ears?
My twin must have them
Earthbound in a fatuous cave
I am oval and contemporary, thin and male
Learning how to self-mother is a necessity
You cannot hemorrhage your way out of it
You may be owed money

It's been a whole year since the last hunt
Time to try a different technique: a floating log

separated from its mother wears a soul-protecting
apron for the afterlife, not an obvious

pursuit of dominance, but a way to keep healthy
and bouncy, although pointless like a floppy disk

used to fan the machinery of the future. If you scroll
too quickly the images become blurry, and who wants

blurry when you can have sleek and nubile elbows.
A pixilated demon gives me monthly migraines

launches me at terrific speeds into survival mode.
I steal my best friend's earthly possessions but not

the earth that goes with it. I pass out from all
the excitement until a feather tickles my anus

and brings me back to life in time to do the wash.
The laundry detergent smells of fresh meadows

but if the liquid is blue you can't see the army
of chemicals invading the children's clothes.

Little does the mother know that we need chemicals
like we need fleas to feast on the troubles of our birth.

Circles make no allowances
not for grievance

or a coughed-up lung
made of soupy vegetables

How do we defend ourselves
from the killing light?

A costume, a corset
squeezes the belly firm

stops the movement of food
through a plastic tube

the sound of atrophy
emerges from a chest

daughters of daughters
promenade down a carpet of

ancient creatures
towards the site of infection

catalyze the people!
disinfect them!

detain them
for years without reason

when the dying is long
it becomes ordinary

another kind of living
that too struggles

under stigma and
obedience

what once was life
is now deposits of mineral water

is now cud
on a silvery spoon

that feeds the baby
in the dingy ménage

Heads of clear-eyed cabbage
await the opening of another portal

It seems simple at the onset
waiting, that is.

A cube of tofu jiggles
on a temple plate

To eat the bird
feathers and all

Their tiny minds
tumbling down a dark tunnel

Now I know why
you are a sad vegetarian

Now I know why
escalators function best

when scaled to the size
of their master riders.

Remember when I rode
the smallest escalator in the world?

I think we were in China
I made myself deliberately small

I stood as still as a mannequin
My pockets stuffed

with wild grasses
and noses of various sizes

Starting at one temperature and unexpectedly
rising to another, the days

Soon lose their purpose. The sunrays
methodically stroke my

Bare ass. My bare ass hides in plain sight.
Special light-producing

Organs help navigate darkened closet spaces.
Gently floating into the darkness.

A room of square tables lures me deeper into my ego.
Birds eat fish and fish eat other fish.

Within a few minutes, all that is left is a shower
of scales. Arranged in

ROYGBIV, and then from largest to smallest.
Defense relies on coordination.

Distribution of life is determined by pre-existing
software. There is no scientific

Explanation for my aggressive behavior.
A creature beats

Its majestic wings, but proves as neither smart
nor effective defense mechanism.

What is it like to be an organism that can only live
within a group of other like-

Minded organisms? Everyday the water gets a little
hotter. Let nothing

Compare to the violence muscled into
the hearts of our youth.

It's a no-win situation, die in the water or die in the air.
Facing little resistance, a feed can be devoured within minutes.
It is impossible to conceal our approach towards living when it

happens before we are born. A breeding hole becomes a depository
for panoptic observations. So much effort for so little food makes
one needy especially in the height of summer. Hypocorisms make

the event more casual, but ultimately leave the day featureless.
True to form, an infection begins in the lungs then travels up the
throat and into the sinuses. Antibodies avoid symmetry, doing

what they can to accommodate the all encompassing view.
Seeking refuge is of no use in the sinewy parts of the body.
What begins with hunger ultimately ends in vengeance.

I paddle ambitiously through the undulating swells of the ocean,
seeking shelter from a whale's enormous maw. There are not
many places to hide when a spotlight follows me everywhere.

The curtain lifts, a cover is blown, and escape seems not only
impossible, but pathetic. Darting from one corner to the next,
I understand what it means to exist solely on the veneer.

I mimic my enemies to make myself more attractive to my suitors.
The bodies of my well-rounded friends will change over time.
I shave all my hairs so that death can slip over my limbs smoothly.

A turquoise pyramid
balances on a band of foam

A computer virus makes
competition more deathy

Hoards of money stashed away
in invisible vaults
don’t hoard money
hoard design

Let death be handy
like adolescent boys
& their pulsating cocks

What once was luxury
is now data
oozing out of pores

manipulated by soft robots
horizontal & perpendicular

at the same time dumb
leaves unfurl into mega leaves

the moon becomes less and less talented

like the deranged totem

outside your lobby window

A wailing woman trapped between two walls
is mistaken for the village ghost
She was the incorrect shape
A village in the shape of a half-buried egg
has no shortcuts
Even if there are no death sticks
Bugs crawl over it
Some of them are blind, but this does not free them
I flip a switch to activate my bug dome.
I hold out my arm and ask: Did I get color?
Depending on the time of day color refers to
pale blue, white, magenta, or gold
A concern for color is a sign of privilege
A room gives birth to another room
A tree birth is not wide enough to hide wires
Hide the baby instead
Never let the young ones be exposed to suffering
A potential for disaster
Child-sized hands reach for me
Luckily my dome rejects them
It is rare to reject an event before it happens
WHAT ARE RARE
I reject my urge to fall into the sleep side
I wail in disbelief

A host of dead trees will not stop being dead for the clamoring
There is intent and then there is fantasy
One can be the Prince of God and still be executed
There is the real world and then there is performance
Baby cries and cries for sunset
Peel back the eyelids
Do not unplug the performance

When co-dependency is the only option, accept exploitation
Adult status means nothing if you have a child's mind
A free spirit, as some girls call it
Dog or fawn
I want to please you all the time
Even while dinner is served
And a plate smashes against my face
The superficial wound heals and becomes
A measly frond in the immense wilderness
The intense urge to flee is not the opposite of servile behavior
Just a different method of escape
It is not the feel, but the aftertaste of experience that determines
Its place on the memory chain
Part dog and/or part fawn
Even the most pure vocabulary cannot subdue the intense urge to flee
A shock to the birds, but not to the natural order of things
I abandon myself recklessly to exhibit my "best behavior"
Being tidy and servile
Is what good girls do best
A good girl is a golden nugget
Like a reusable stamp
Or velcro on a shoe strap
Recognition of talents, obscure as they are
Begins with who you know

Then making sure that the people you know tell the people they
know about you
And so on and so forth
Rosily down the chain of command
Into the dungeon
If communication is not your strong suit
Then try again
Try harder
Dissolve all boundaries
A spirit can easily slip in between cage bars
Seeks safety by merging with the wishes of other spirits
Give way to flattery at the first sign of a perceived threat
At least one of you is a narcissist
At least one of you is a dog

All creatures have one thing in common:
Exploiting the good times so they can endure the bad

Desperation can lead animals to do dangerous things
like sitting around in bed all day motionless, watching

the computer change colors while predators peer through
the kitchen window. What is wrong with you to lead you

to believe that there are snakes in the mint box? A frenzied
search is made more complex by the lack of chase room

so you navigate a labyrinth of melt holes without making
a sound. The practice of putting animals in your mouth

is neither shameful nor climactic as long as it enhances
your vision. A herd has many eyes. The predator instinctively

moves the prize out of sight. At home a mother slobbers all over
the faces of her cubs. In bed my lover slobbers all over my wound.

Request accommodations to lessen the shock of disappearance
Once beneath the mirrory surface, we will all be forced to drown.

A hunt agile and unworthy conflicts with
what nature should be

A pulsating network of powerful currents
constantly on the move

Outside forces cross whole oceans
Seek to destroy what is male

Sometimes you cannot know how things
begin or die when new species

suddenly appear over the course of centuries
and are forced to crawl on their hands

and knees towards safety.
A greenhouse for invasives conflict with

what nature should be:
Submissive, indifferent, and unwarranted.

Threatened with extinction, people of a nation dig
a tunnel to cross a border, an impenetrable mass

of muscle and horn. On the other side of the mass,
fruit and candied violets await children,

expectant mothers, fireman, travelers, pilgrims
and aborted babies.

Migration becomes far more difficult when there
are no signs of habitation, no trees in sight,

and predators. The predators lurk in limbo for
what feels like eternity.

Reminded of their brutality, expectant mothers
and common brides take shelter in unseeing trees.

Their fates sealed by connective tissue and fertile
hips, naturally internally rotated.

Insertion happens where you least expect it
A modicum of disbelief can throw an entire operation off balance
First locate the feminine in the hierarchy of needs
How can you set standards for arousal when you are so far ahead of your time?
What is the feminine form for the word *arousal*?
The loss of self before words is a testament to a life of labor
Lonely soggy fruit spoils in purgatory while
Finicky ships pass the summits of underwater mountains in the night
Some of us are cross-eyed and starving
Not all of us
Some of us cry and cry into the camera
In hopes of gaining sympathy
Exhibitionists be frank and ruined
How long does it take for rumors to spread in the golden meadow?
And what are the grammatical genders of these rumors?
Drink orange flower water to prepare for the operation
Most of the time we are hanging out saving energy
In an open field of light
Where parents make your apparitions come to life
And force you to perform even when you don't want to
Weaving an intricate web of lies
Deception must be at the heart of
Disease hiding in plain sight
A tail chase brings you back to the starting point

After running circles around
Where insertion begins
And ends
In the familiar plain
Beside the familiar sea

I. COMMUNITY GARDEN FOR LONELY GIRLS

II. FAMILY TEACHINGS

III. MEN DYING FOR WEALTH, BIRDS DYING FOR FOODS

IV. THE APPARITION

IN "SO MUCH ABUNDANCE DOES NOT GO UNNOTICED"

the italicized line *The religious fear of evil can itself lead to evil* is from Jia Tolentino's essay "What Happens When We Decide Everyone Else is a Narcissist," published in the *New Yorker*

THE TITLE SECTIONS IN "FAMILY TEACHINGS"

are from *A Lost Tribe*, by Ming-Tung Hsieh

IN "FAMILY TEACHINGS"

the lines *The ancient Chinese believe the spirit of all dead ancestors must be catered so as to avoid any angry ghosts in the family*, and *To have no lineage will be without the basic social protection* are also from *A Lost Tribe*, by Ming-Tung Hsieh

IN "DYING IS EASIEST WHEN DONE ALONE"

the italicized line *when the dying is long it becomes ordinary* is from Larissa MacFarquhar's essay "A Tender Hand in the Presence of Death," published in the *New Yorker*

IN "A HISTORY OF DETAINMENT"

the italicized line: t*he mound is oddly precise* is from Brandon Shimoda's essay "Notes for National Corpse Month, Part Two," published on the Harriet Blog at the Poetry Foundation

Thank you to the editors of the following literary publications where earlier versions of some of these poems have appeared: *Belladonna**, *Bone Bouquet*, *Dusie*, *EOAGH*, *Elderly*, *Fanzine*, *Ilk*, *iO Poetry*, *La Vague Journal*, *Lemon Hound*, *NOÖ*, and *Poor Claudia*.

A special thanks to Miles Frieden, Arlo Haskell, and Dara Wier at the Key West Literary Seminar for the opportunity to share a selection of these poems with the Key West community.

I am very grateful for Ben Estes and Alan Felsenthal at The Song Cave for publishing a selection of these poems in the chapbook: "I'm Sunlight" (The Song Cave, 2016).

Thank you to Drew Scott Swenhaugen for his editorial oversight and guidance.
Thank you to Brenda Iijima for starting the conversation.

And finally, love and deep gratitude to Austin Alter, Cindy Arrieu-King, Diana Khoi Nguyen, Patricia No, and Brandon Shimoda for the continued collaborations, friendship, and support. You are my foundation.